EIGHT ROUNDS

for 3 flutes and optional piano

Joachim Johow

Order number: DHP 1084486-400

Eight Rounds for 3 Flutes and Optional Piano
Joachim Johow

ISBN 978-90-431-2974-9
NUR 472

CD number: DHR 13-631-3
CD recorded by: De Haske Sound Services BV

© **Copyright 2008 by De Haske Publications BV,**
Postbus 744, NL-8440 AS Heerenveen, Holland
Voor België / Pour la Belgique : De Haske Belgium BVBA, B-1860 Meise
Für Deutschland: De Haske (Deutschland) GmbH, Postfach 51, D-79427 Eschbach
Pour la France : De Haske France, B.P. 69, F-68180 Horbourg-Wihr
Per l'Italia: De Haske Italia s.r.l., Centro Direzionale Milanofiori, Palazzo E/3, I-20090 Assago (MI)
For Japan: De Haske Japan Co., Ltd., 2-10-5 Ningyocho, Nihonbashi, Chuoku, Tokyo 103-0013, Japan
Für Österreich: Musikverlag De Haske GmbH, A-6884 Damüls
Für die Schweiz / Pour la Suisse : De Haske (International) AG, Postfach 60, CH-6332 Hagendorn
For the UK: De Haske Music (UK) Ltd, Fleming Road, Earlstrees, Corby, Northants NN17 4SN, England
All other countries: De Haske Publications BV, Postbus 744, NL-8440 AS Heerenveen, Holland

All rights reserved. No part of this book may be reproduced in any form, by print, photocopy, microfilm, or any other means without written permission of the publisher.

Alle Rechte vorbehalten. Vervielfältigung und/oder Veröffentlichung dieses Buches, auch einzelner Teile, mittels Druck, Fotokopie, Mikrofilm etc. ohne schriftliche Einwilligung des Herausgebers verboten.

Tous droits réservés pour tous pays. Aucune partie de ce livre ne peut être reproduite sous aucune forme : imprimée, photocopiée, microfilmée ou par tout autre moyen sans l'autorisation de l'éditeur.

Tutti i diritti riservati. Nessuna parte di questo libro puo' essere riprodotta sotto alcuna forma, stampata, fotocopiata, microfilmata, ecc., senza l'autorizzazione scritta dell'editore.

Alle rechten voorbehouden. Niets van deze uitgave mag worden verveelvoudigd en/of openbaar gemaakt door middel van druk, fotokopie, microfilm of op welke andere wijze dan ook zonder voorafgaande schriftelijke toestemming van de uitgever.

Printed in Holland.

EIGHT ROUNDS
for 3 flutes and optional piano

CONTENTS - INHALT - SOMMAIRE - INHOUD

CD track no.

1. **TUNING NOTE A**
2. **MONDAY SONG** 8
3. **ROUND FOR EDVARD** 9
4. **THREE BIKES** 10
5. **THE KING OF THE FAIRIES IS COMIN'** 12
6. **TALKING FLUTES** 14
7. **SWINGING MINUET** 16
8. **TIPTOE CATS** 18
9. **A LITTLE ROUND** 19

EIGHT ROUNDS

for 3 flutes and optional piano

FOREWORD

Don't we all know rounds? No matter whether they are cheerful or sad, new or old – everybody likes them! This collection of rounds for three flutes and optional piano (bass *ad lib.*) contains eight modern rounds in various styles. With this book you can enhance and enrich your music lessons in many ways.

Effective learning from playing rounds:
By playing rounds, students can practise sight-reading together, and learn to hold a part independently. Rounds are also good for teaching young beginners, as they learn a great deal by imitation.

Varied and creative uses of these rounds:
Rounds are ideal warm-up pieces for group lessons, leading from monophony to polyphony. The rounds collected in this book can also be accompanied by a staged performance (for example with dancing and acting) – giving rise to a varied and highly motivational lesson plan. The results of your class work will certainly be appreciated by the audience in concerts and school performances!

Thanks to the piano accompaniment in the appendix you can accompany your students yourself, or use the piano accompaniment on the enclosed CD.

Have great fun with *Eight Rounds*!

Notes for the performance:
If weaker players are not able to play the whole round, let them play the first section only, during the final play through.

It is advisable to begin with everyone playing the whole round all together. Following this, the round could be played in two parts (for example with the teacher playing one part); finally, the round should be played in three parts.

Joachim Johow
Joachim Johow was born in Berlin in 1952 and later studied at the conservatory there. After performing (violin), his passion was composing. During his studies he became acquainted with Irish, Hungarian and Yiddish music and the expressiveness, vitality and sensitivity found in these musical traditions made a deep impression on him.

He was the leader of a klezmer orchestra in Berlin for over ten years. During this time he came into contact with the famous clarinettist Giora Feidman, who performed together with Johow and played his music.

In addition to composing pieces inspired by folk music Johow has written many works for various ensembles and orchestras. He works as a music teacher and still lives in Berlin.

EIGHT ROUNDS
for 3 flutes and optional piano

VORWORT

Wer kennt keine Kanons? Egal, ob lustig oder traurig, neu oder alt – sie machen einfach jedem Spaß! Die vorliegende Sammlung von Kanons für drei Flöten und optionales Klavier (Bass *ad lib.*) enthält acht moderne Kanons in unterschiedlichen Stilen. Mit diesem Buch können Sie Ihren Unterricht in vielerlei Hinsicht bereichern und vertiefen.

Der Lerneffekt durch das Kanon spielen ist hoch:
Beim Einstudieren von Kanons können die Schüler das gemeinsame Vom-Blatt-Spiel üben und lernen außerdem das selbstständige Halten einer Stimme. Kanons eignen sich auch wunderbar für den Anfängerunterricht von Kindern, da diese sehr gut durch Imitation zum Musizieren kommen.

Die Einsatzmöglichkeiten dieser Kanons sind vielfältig und kreativ:
Kanons sind die idealen Einspielstücke für den Gruppenunterricht, da sie von der Einstimmigkeit in die Polyphonie führen. Die Kanons in diesem Buch eignen sich darüber hinaus auch zur szenischen Umsetzung (z. B. mit Tanz und Darstellung), was der abwechslungsreichen, hoch motivierenden Unterrichtsgestaltung viel Raum bietet. Und das Ergebnis der Arbeit kann sich dann bei Konzerten und Klassenvorspielen sicherlich hören und sehen lassen!

Dank der Klavierstimme im Anhang können Sie Ihre Schüler selbst begleiten oder die Klavierbegleitung auf der beiliegenden CD nutzen.

Wir wünschen viel Spaß mit *Eight Rounds*!

Anmerkungen zum Vortrag:
Sollte eine Stimme von schwächeren Spielern nicht durchgehend gespielt werden können, reicht es, wenn diese im letzten Einsatz nur den ersten Teil spielen.

Natürlich sollte am Anfang das gemeinsame Durchspielen des gesamten Kanons stehen. Danach kann das zweistimmige Spiel (in dem z. B. der Lehrer/die Lehrerin eine Stimme spielt) folgen und dann schließlich die dreistimmige Fassung erklingen.

Joachim Johow
Joachim Johow wurde 1952 in Berlin geboren. Er studierte dort an der Hochschule für Musik. Neben dem Musizieren (Violine) wurde das Komponieren zu seiner Leidenschaft. Während seiner Studienzeit kam er in Kontakt mit irischer, ungarischer und jiddischer Musik, deren Ausdrucksstärke, Vitalität und Sensibilität ihn tief beeindruckte.

Joachim Johow leitete mehr als zehn Jahre lang ein Klezmerorchester in Berlin. In diese Zeit fällt auch der Kontakt zum berühmten Klarinettisten Giora Feidman, der zusammen mit Johow auftrat und dessen Musik spielte.

Neben der Komposition von folkloristisch inspirierten Stücken, verfasste Joachim Johow zahlreiche Werke für verschiedene Ensembles und Orchester. Derzeit ist er als Musiklehrer tätig und lebt mit seiner Familie in Berlin.

EIGHT ROUNDS
for 3 flutes and optional piano

PRÉFACE

Chacun d'entre nous connaît au moins un canon. Qu'ils soient joyeux ou mélancoliques, anciens ou récents, les canons font l'unanimité. Ce recueil contient huit canons modernes pour trois flûtes traversières et piano optionnel (basse *ad lib.*), écrits dans des styles variés. *Eight Rounds* ("Huit canons") est un excellent moyen d'enrichir et de dynamiser vos cours.

Apprendre efficacement en jouant des canons :
Le jeu en canon permet aux élèves de travailler ensemble la lecture à vue et d'apprendre à tenir sa voix/partie de façon indépendante. Les canons sont également un excellent outil d'apprentissage basé sur l'imitation. Cela est particulièrement vrai pour les très jeunes débutants.

Utiliser les canons de façon variée et créative :
Le canon est un exercice d'échauffement idéal pour un cours d'ensemble (mutation de la monophonie à la polyphonie). Les canons réunis dans ce recueil peuvent être accompagnés d'une mise en scène (théâtre ou danse). Ils forment alors un plan de cours très motivant et divertissant. Et lorsque vous présenterez votre travail en concert ou en audition, il recevra sans aucun doute un accueil chaleureux du public.

Vous trouverez en annexe une version papier de l'accompagnement de piano. Vous pouvez accompagner vous-même vos élèves ou utiliser l'accompagnement de piano enregistré sur le compact disc inclus.

Nous vous souhaitons beaucoup de plaisir à l'interprétation de ces huit canons.

Conseils d'interprétation :
Si les élèves les plus faibles n'ont pas les capacités pour tenir une partie en entier, proposez leur de jouer uniquement la première voix, du début jusqu'à l'entrée du deuxième flûtiste.

Nous vous conseillons de commencer par faire jouer chaque canon par le groupe entier. Après cette première lecture en groupe, jouez les canons à deux voix (le professeur se charge de jouer une des deux voix), puis à trois voix.

Joachim Johow
Né en 1952 à Berlin, Joachim Johow reçoit une formation musicale approfondie au Conservatoire de sa ville natale. Parallèlement à ses activités de violoniste, il développe une passion pour la composition. Pendant ses études, il se familiarise avec les musiques hongroise, irlandaise et yiddish. L'expressivité, la vitalité et la sensibilité que l'on trouve dans ces traditions musicales ont profondément impressionné le compositeur.

Joachim Johow a été le leader d'un orchestre klezmer berlinois pendant plus de dix ans. Au cours de cette période, il fait la connaissance du célèbre clarinettiste Giora Friedman qui l'accompagnera et interprétera ses compositions.

Joachim Johow a composé des œuvres inspirées de musiques traditionnelles et des pièces pour divers ensembles et formations orchestrales. Actuellement, il vit et enseigne à Berlin.

EIGHT ROUNDS
for 3 flutes and optional piano

VOORWOORD

We kennen allemaal wel een aantal canons. En of ze nu vrolijk of droevig, nieuw of oud zijn – het is altijd genieten geblazen! Deze bundel voor drie fluiten en een optionele pianobegeleiding (bas *ad lib.*) bevat acht moderne canons in diverse stijlen. Met dit boek kunt u uw muzieklessen in veel opzichten verrijken en verdiepen.

Effectief leren met canons
Bij het instuderen van canons kunnen leerlingen het noten lezen samen oefenen. Bovendien leren ze hun eigen partij zelfstandig vast te houden. Canons zijn ook geschikt voor het onderwijs aan jonge beginners, want zij leren veel door te imiteren.

Gevarieerde en creatieve toepassingen
Canons zijn ideale stukken voor de warming-up in groepslessen, aangezien ze van eenstemmig naar meerstemmig spel leiden. De canons in dit boek lenen zich ook uitstekend voor een scènische uitvoering (bijvoorbeeld met dans en toneelspel) – waarmee ruimte ontstaat voor een veelzijdig en zeer motiverend lestraject. De resultaten van uw lessen zullen bij optredens en voorspeelavonden beslist worden gewaardeerd door het publiek.

Dankzij de pianopartijen in de bijlage kunt u zelf uw studenten begeleiden, maar u kunt er ook voor kiezen de pianobegeleidingen te gebruiken die op de bijgevoegde cd staan.

Veel plezier met *Eight Rounds*!

Aanwijzingen voor de uitvoering
Als wat minder goede spelers een partij niet helemaal uit kunnen spelen, kunt u ze als laatste laten inzetten en alleen het eerste stukje (tot aan cijfer 2) laten spelen.

Het is raadzaam om eerst de hele canon eenstemmig door iedereen te laten doorspelen. Daarna kunt u de canon eventueel in twee partijen verdelen (en bijvoorbeeld zelf een partij voor uw rekening nemen); ten slotte is het de bedoeling dat de canon driestemmig wordt gespeeld.

Joachim Johow
Joachim Johow werd in 1952 in Berlijn geboren, waar hij aan het conservatorium studeerde. Naast het musiceren op de viool werd het componeren zijn passie. Tijdens zijn studie leerde hij Ierse, Hongaarse en Jiddische muziek kennen; hij was diep onder de indruk van de expressie, vitaliteit en melancholie ervan.

Ruim tien jaar lang leidde hij een klezmerorkest in Berlijn. In die periode kwam hij in contact met de beroemde klarinettist Giora Feidman, die samen met Johow optrad en zijn muziek speelde.

Behalve op volksmuziek gebaseerde stukken heeft Johow veel werken geschreven voor diverse ensembles en orkesten. Verder werkt hij momenteel als muziekdocent en is hij nog steeds woonachtig in Berlijn.

MONDAY SONG

Joachim Johow

© Copyright 2008 by **De Haske (International) AG**

ROUND FOR EDVARD

Joachim Johow

THREE BIKES

Track 4

♩ = 142

Joachim Johow

THREE BIKES

Track 5

THE KING OF THE FAIRIES IS COMIN'

♩ = 100

Joachim Johow

THE KING OF THE FAIRIES IS COMIN'

Track

TALKING FLUTES

Joachim Johow

▶ 1

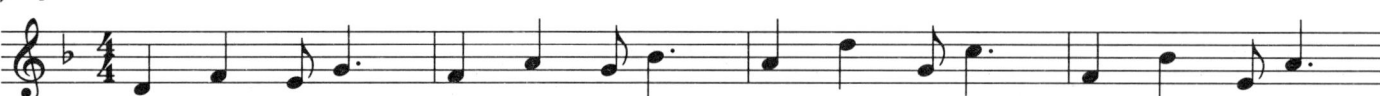

▶ 2

TALKING FLUTES

SWINGING MINUET

Joachim Johow

SWINGING MINUET

TIPTOE CATS

Joachim Johow

A LITTLE ROUND

Track 9

♩ = 140

Joachim Johow

• ALL TIME KLEZMERS

This is a wonderful collection of klezmer music, inspired by the Jewish dances and songs of the klezmorim from Eastern Europe: from the lyrical *Hora* to the fast, compelling *Freilach*. Also audible is the influence of more recent Israeli folk music à la Giora Feidman. Some of the pieces have a second part ad libitum – for playing together or for variation in a repeat. For the accompaniment, chord symbols have been added, and on the enclosed CD there are complete versions as well as play-along versions of all pieces, played live by genuine klezmer musicians.

Order no.   1245-05-400 DHI

Joachim Johow

• SWING QUARTETS
JAZZ QUARTETS
GROOVE QUARTETS

Form a fantastic, swinging quartet with three flute colleagues! Or you may choose to use a *Swing Quartet* book to form a combination and play together with other instruments, such as the clarinet, saxophone and trumpet. This will make the music sound really jazzy.
Each piece is recorded on the CD six times. The first time you'll hear the combo and the four parts as a whole; then follow four versions in which respectively the first, second, third, and fourth parts have been left out; and finally, you'll hear a version with just the combo.
With the combo accompaniment books you can also play all quartets with your own band. They contain the accompaniment parts for piano, guitar, bass and drums – for a complete rhythm group to accompany the wind players.

	Quartet book	Combo accompaniment book
Swing Quartets	DHP 1053535-400	DHP 1074358-401
Jazz Quartets	DHP 1053956-400	DHP 1074359-401
Groove Quartets	DHP 1064153-400	DHP 1074360-401